formal ponds
and water gardens

formal ponds
and water gardens

Philip Swindells

BARRON'S

First edition for the United States and Canada
published in 2002 by Barron's Educational Series, Inc.

First published in 2002 by Interpet Publishing.
© Copyright 2002 by Interpet Publishing.

All inquiries should be addressed to:
Barron's Educational Series, Inc.
250 Wireless Boulevard
Hauppauge, NY 11788
www.barronseduc.com

International Standard Book No. 0-7641-1846-3

Library of Congress Catalog Card No. 2001095378

THE AUTHOR
Philip Swindells is a water gardening specialist with a
long experience of growing aquatic plants in many
parts of the world. He trained at the University of
Cambridge Botanic Garden and the famous aquatic
nursery of Perrys of Enfield, and ultimately became
Curator of Harlow Carr Botanical Gardens, Harrogate.
The author of many publications on water gardening,
Philip was also formerly the editor of the *Water Garden
Journal* of the International Water lily Society, who in
1994 inducted him into their Hall of Fame. He was
awarded a Mary Hellier Scholarship in 1990 by the
International Plant Propagator's Society for pioneering
work on the propagation of water lilies.

Acknowledgments
The publishers would like to thank the
following people and companies who provided
much appreciated help and advice during the
preparation of this book: "G" at Old Barn
Nurseries, Dial Post, Horsham; Hillhout Ltd for
providing timber for photography; Murrells
Nursery, Pulborough, West Sussex; and Stuart
Thraves at Blagdon, Bridgwater, Somerset.

Printed in China
9 8 7 6 5 4 3 2 1

contents

introduction

The formal water garden has a long and fascinating history. Developing out of the need to bring irrigation water to crops, it has become an important part of gardening fashion in the 21st century. Formal water features originated in the Middle and East East and were initially associated with warm or mild climates; from there they moved north through the Mediterranean countries before extending into northern Europe and North America.

Although originally functional, formal pools have evolved into both focal points and reflective features in the garden. Whereas plants are sometimes used to enhance the formal effect, pools are often totally devoid of aquatic life and exist merely to mirror the surroundings. Formal water is also used to create landscape illusions. A garden that is foreshortened can be successfully lengthened visually by constructing a narrow pool or canal that in perspective appears to be parallel-sided but in reality is slightly narrower at the distant end.

Rills and canals are all connected with formal water, often being used to link separate features. Narrow rills especially can be used to great effect around the garden. Not only do they divide a plot conveniently but they serve to lead the visitor on—for we all have a great affinity with moving water and a desire to follow it wherever it goes.

The sound of a trickling rill is also soothing, and the silvery swirl of water as it travels on its way creates life and movement.

Moving water is an important element in many formal water gardens. Although fountains are often seen "playing" in informal pools, the only natural forms of moving water are streams and waterfalls. In a formal situation, the element of artifice by which water is tossed into the air can become a positive feature of the design. Imitation of nature is not the restrictive criterion that it can be in the creation of informal pools.

The fountain that throws water into the air in various spray patterns is probably the most widely enjoyed type of fountain. The feature is very simply created with a submersible pump and fountain attachment. The pump only needs to be placed in the pool and the power connected, and everything swings at once into action. Likewise the modern pump has transformed waterfalls, cascades, and water staircases into easily created features.

Formal water, although essentially simple in nature, does require careful maintenance if it is to look its best. Even though there may be no plants or fish in the pool, it still needs regular attention. But this is not an onerous task, and it ensures that the water feature retains its place as the jewel in the crown of the modern garden.

Above: *A formal water feature looks best in suitably formal surroundings.*
Right: *A formal pond often depends on the reflective quality of the water for its visual success. Here plants are absent from the water, but they make an important contribution to the setting through which the water flows.*

classical-style square pools

The classical formal pool originated in Greece and Italy. Like the traditional Moorish and Arabic styles, it grew out of a need to irrigate crops in a reliable way. Usually, the spring from where the water originated became an early kind of water garden, a temple honoring a god or goddess perhaps being constructed nearby. Trees were planted and, in time, a garden added. As more elaborate channels and basins arose, statues were added—not only to ornament but to propel water in jets or streams.

The Romans incorporated the best elements of the Greek pleasure garden into their villa gardens, and the use of water for purely decorative purposes was born. Aqueducts and fountains were used freely, and many are still functioning in the great cities of Italy. The channels and rills of the Greeks and Italians developed into canal-like ponds, and influences from India and the Far East led to the establishment of square and rectangular ponds, often with seating areas within them. These were great for countries with very hot weather. Many of these island-like seating places were linked by stepping-stones, the pond being used primarily for recreation rather than visual appeal.

Right: *Ponds like this originally arose from the need to irrigate a garden, but eventually they became ornamental centerpieces in their own right. The upright conifers lend a Mediterranean feel to the garden scene and reflect the period when formally arranged trees were often associated with water.*

Below left: *An unplanted canal-like pool with a formally planted waterside. The open water is intended to reflect everything around it, while at the same time providing an illusion of distance within the garden. Many pools of this type narrow at the far end, to give an illusion of distance to a small plot.*

Left: *An attractive formal arrangement. The paved area and pool are in proportion to one another, and the symmetrically arranged clumps of aquatic irises stand guard alongside the fountain mask.*

Modern square or rectangular pools are generally constructed to fit into the garden landscape. The pool shape reflects the contours of those parts of the garden that lie adjacent, whether they be bed, border, or lawn. Many of these pools are constructed to serve as mirrors, the water reflecting the garden in its glassy stillness. They are rarely planted, except for one or two clumps of strategically placed water lilies and perhaps some spiky reeds bristling in the corners.

classical-style round pools

There is no reliable precedent for the circular or curved pool, although both probably evolved from the Greek nymphaeum—a grotto or shrine sacred to the nymphs. Throughout history, circular and curved pools have appeared in garden design, the circular ones typically used primarily to reflect the sky and the curved ones to delineate other parts of the garden or to house fountains or fountain statuary.

Fountains can be incorporated into circular pools too, and one of the most impressive sights in the formal garden is a circular pool with a single jet of water arising from its center. A pool devoid of plants and highlighted by a silvery plume of water twisting in the bright sunlight has a magic all of its own.

Circular pools, unlike square and rectangular ones, usually stand alone. Classical styles generally have a raised surround with elaborate ornamentation, and this effect can be achieved by using one of the fine reconstituted stone products that are sold in garden centers nowadays. Available in sectional form, they are easily assembled and have much of the grandeur associated with the historic gardens.

Similarly many of the fountain ornaments of classical design for circular ponds are faithful, although scaled-down, reproductions of famous fountains and lend a touch of majesty to the most modest plot.

Right: *This circular pool is greatly enhanced by the wider circle of neatly arranged pavers. This enables the pool to retain its air of formality, despite the cluttered arrangement of floating and marginal plants.*

Below: *Raised ponds that are symmetrical usually rest quite easily in the garden landscape.*

Right: *This simple circular raised pond is the focal point of the entire garden. So much depends upon its proportions and planting arrangement for the overall picture to be a success. The containers reflect the shape of the pond and themselves make circular contributions to a garden dominated by circles. The two small trees stand as sentinels guarding the approach to the pond from the outer garden.*

raised pools

There are a number of reasons, apart from purely aesthetic ones, why it is desirable to have a raised pool. On a conventional level site, height can be a useful design asset. It also provides the fish with greater protection from predator animals. There is some merit also in the fact that it is difficult for children to tumble into the water accidentally, although if a low wall is part of the pool, this may prove a tempting attraction for children who will want to run along it.

A raised pool that is contained by a conventional wall is a fascinating feature, for it brings the pool nearer to the observer. There are few greater pleasures in a garden than to sit on the edge of a raised pool on a warm summer day dabbling one's fingers in the cool water and observing the fish as they glide effortlessly beneath verdant water lily pads.

Below: This is quite a simple pool to construct. Here concrete blockwork has been attractively rendered with a cement mix.

Above: *This pool is an important decorative feature in its garden. Plants are important, but visually the pool would benefit from fewer plants so that the clear water surface could be enjoyed more.*

Although raised pools can be desirable in themselves, they can also serve to link parts of the garden that are at differing levels. Rather than the conventional stream or waterfall, raised pools of varying heights can link levels in a terracing effect, water tumbling from one to another. Even still water contained at different levels provides a visual link. Raised pool features can even be recessed into a slope and slightly raised above it; where appropriate, steps can be incorporated in the same way as one might in a conventional terraced garden feature.

A sloping site also provides an opportunity for using innovative formal designs where triangles, rhomboids, and parallelograms can be incorporated comfortably into an overall garden scheme. For the most part, it is only in the formal garden with a sloping aspect that such configurations rest easy.

oriental-style water gardens

The Oriental style of gardening uses water freely. Although nowadays most gardeners associate it with Japanese gardening, it was the Chinese who first developed the theme many centuries ago, when it migrated to Japan as Buddhism spread. Chinese art forms, including garden design, reached Japan in the 6th and 7th centuries A.D. The Chinese influence gradually declined, and by the 17th century a distinctive Japanese style, which borrowed the original theme of man's relationship with nature from the Chinese, had evolved. This style was more precise and symbolic, and came largely from Zen Buddhist monks.

Below: *Everything in this Oriental garden is positioned precisely and with meaning. The rocks represent mountains, the trees forests, and the pool a lake. The seat is positioned in an ideal place for quiet contemplation and personal reflection.*

Oriental gardens use water to add beauty and tranquillity and to create a place where people can contemplate and observe nature and discover their place in the natural order. A calm, reflecting surface of water is intended to expand one's sense of peace and create an atmosphere conducive to thought. Besides putting the observer in the right frame of mind, the Oriental water feature is intended to guide the visitor through the garden by linking together its various parts. As in the natural world, the garden should hold mysteries that slowly unravel as the path of the winding stream is followed. Water, rocks, and plants are elaborately arranged into what amounts to a real life representation of a landscape painting.

In the domestic garden, the best visual parts of the Oriental theme are usually appropriated and used, and then planted liberally with appropriate Asiatic plants. The Oriental influence may extend no further than to a visual look. The Japanese and Chinese passion for shaped rocks and raked gravel finds little favor in the West, but their overall designs for open water are proving to be increasingly popular.

Left: *A wonderful interpretation of an Oriental water garden. Peace and tranquillity pervade the atmosphere, helped immeasurably by the presence of water. The bamboo* shishi-odoshi *in the background with its gentle splash of water brings a natural sound to the scene.*

moorish and arabic-style water gardens

The Moorish and Arabic styles of water gardening have grown out of the need for ancient civilizations in warm climates to be able to water their crops reliably. The irrigation channels of Egypt and Mesopotamia were developed many centuries ago, and they led to the formality seen in Moorish and Arabic gardens, where they also evolved into a formal decorative arrangement. This can be seen in the magnificent Mosque of Cordoba in Spain, where rows of orange trees are planted to complement the features both aesthetically and practically. It is probably the oldest continuously maintained water garden in the world.

The Persians, who had similar environmental conditions, developed the irrigation theme further, treating water in the garden rather like an oasis. This reflected the natural human desire to shelter oneself from the inhospitable desert. The traditional Persian garden, known as *chahar bagh*, was a fourfold garden. It consisted of a level, enclosed garden divided into four squares by two canals crossing in the center. A pool, fountain, or pavilion was usually positioned in the center. The canals radiating from this point represented the four rivers of paradise, and both flowers and fruit were planted heavily around them.

It was these elements of design that the Arabs who conquered Persia in the 7th century took back and incorporated in their creations. These ideas were widely embraced, as the layout coincided with the descriptions of the garden of paradise found in the Koran.

Traditionally the Moorish and Arabic styles of gardening have symbolized earthly paradise, and water has played an important central role in this, even to the extent that water flows from within buildings to pools and channels outdoors. Water is central to the theme of retreat, contemplation, and pleasure.

Above: *Water plays an important part in the Arabic-style garden. The rill is a legacy from a time when water for irrigation was channeled into the garden.*

Above: *This spectacular formal arrangement in the Arabic style demonstrates the wealth and importance of its owner. Designs of this kind are taken from a period when the detail and intricacy of the construction were directly related to the power and wealth of the commissioning patron.*

Left: *A quiet courtyard garden where the raised central pool provides a focal point. In warm climates, such an arrangement creates a cool ambience.*

the 21st-century look

The 21st century has brought with it a plethora of interesting and bizarre innovations. Television makeover programs have contributed, in no small measure, to a kind of garden theater that is to be applauded for the manner in which it has popularized the use of water in the garden, but that should be regarded with caution when considering the longevity of some designs. Not that the structures created are necessarily ephemeral, but the materials that are used have not been tested for any extended period in the garden, so their use is inevitably something of a step into the unknown.

Wood, metal, and mirrors are all used extensively to create a modern look, and at first sight they are unlikely companions for water when regarded in the traditional manner. However, there is no reason why they should not be used successfully, particularly when combined fashionably with tall-growing architectural plants, both in the water and at the poolside.

Wood has previously normally been used in its rustic form to edge a pool or contain a bog garden. Now it can be fearlessly used in a contemporary style, and sawed, planed, and adorned with colorful preservatives. It can be transformed into a raised pool feature, for creating walkways

Below: A fine example of a water feature where plants would be an intrusion. The modern design is quite capable of standing alone.

Left: *A successful combination of a traditional mask with modern materials in a very futuristic formal arrangement.*

Below: *In the 21st century, celebrity is everything, and images of personalities now find their way into the water garden.*

and decking, as well as for a tumbling formal waterfall or chute. Metal is harder to work with, but it too finds its way into the modern pool as a chromium-plated reflective feature or as tubes and pipes arranged in elaborate or playful configuration.

Mirrors and glass are used to reflect water and the surrounding garden. When they are combined with lighting, the effects can be quite spectacular. Add moving water and, if you wish, synchronized music to accompany it, and you will have encapsulated the way that water gardening is moving purposefully into the 21st century.

moving water in formal features

Moving water is an important part of many formal water gardens. Plants typically play a minor role, and the water is appreciated more for its intrinsic aesthetic value than for sustaining the life of beautiful aquatic plants. Indeed, many aquatic plants, like water lilies and water hawthorn, find it difficult to live with moving water, because they naturally prosper in quiet still backwaters.

Moving water takes three main forms: a fountain; a cascade or waterfall; or a rill or canal. In the latter case rills and channels usually form the structure and backbone of the garden, being arranged in formal geometrical patterns to divide the garden into areas or beds. The channel is also a device for leading the visitor from one place to another, the desire to follow moving water being virtually irresistible.

Above: *This slender ribbon of water divides the garden and permits water to flow with geometric precision. Such rills are also used to lead the visitor subtly from one part of the garden to another.*

Left: *A modern interpretation of the traditional water staircase. The gentle tumbling of a sheet of water over well-placed steps adds movement and delicate sound to a quiet garden scene. Such features require regular cleaning and removal of algal deposits.*

Waterfalls and cascades are usually combined with chutes to create curtains or even formal distributions of water tumbling over a smooth edge. The curtain of water, when properly executed, is particularly fine, especially when positioned to catch streaming sunlight. Light is also important for a fountain. A dull, poorly lit site does it no justice. In the formal water garden, the fountain can be

Above: *A clever way of introducing moving water into a formal garden. It is visually appealing and quite safe for children.*

regarded as a liquid sculpture with a life and movement of its own. Its display can be simply varied by regulating the water outflow control of the submersible pump or choosing alternative fountain jet nozzles.

fountain features

Fountains are wonderful additions to the formal pool, especially where plants are absent and the emphasis is solely on the sculptural quality of the water. Full rein can then be given to the imagination, the only constraint being the splash of the fountain and where the breeze may take it. Providing the tumbling spray can be contained within the pool, anything is possible.

Fountains come in an array of configurations. Some are gushing with white aerated water, others are gently falling, swaying curtains. All the effects are produced by the size and configuration of the fountain jet nozzle, rather than

Below: *Fountains need not produce tall elaborate spray patterns. The smaller gusher fountain is equally attractive, especially in a confined, heavily planted space, such as is pictured here.*

Above: *The elegance of moving water arching into the air and falling in formal patterns. When selecting such a fountain, make sure that the spray height is in proportion to the surroundings.*

the pump itself. Modern submersible pumps are all very similar, differing principally in the amount of water that they can deliver. They can be positioned almost anywhere, either on the floor of the pool or on a specially constructed raised plinth. Varying fountain heads can be used in order to create a great range of jets and spray patterns, most

catalogs providing illustrations of the available options.

Fountains are usually placed in the pool where they are visually balanced with the other elements. If there are no plants, then a filter attached to the pump unit can be very useful in ensuring that much of the organic dust and debris that accumulates is captured. Suspended algae can also be taken out by using a filter connected to the pump, and the display can be enhanced by using underwater lighting with a fountain.

formal planted pools

A formal pool can be planted as liberally as an informal one and look very fine, but for most gardeners the purpose of having a formal water feature is to enjoy the water in its own right, as much as the prospect of cultivating aquatic plants. So the planting arrangements of formal pools are generally more restrained and typically very symmetrical. Consideration is rarely given to creating a natural ecobalance in the pool, for it is difficult to produce a formal effect that is pleasing to the eye and at the same time have all the plant components necessary to ensure a balanced ecology.

Submerged plants are not essential to the well-being of a pool that is being managed artificially by chemicals, but they do make a major contribution. They produce life-giving oxygen and mop up excessive nutrients, thereby depriving suspended algae of a livelihood.

Floating plants, so popular in informal arrangements, find little favor with formal plantings. Surface leaf forms and blossoms are mostly provided by water lilies or other deep-water aquatics, such as water hawthorn (*Aponogeton distachyos*) and water fringe (*Nymphoides peltata*). However, when there is moving water, especially the splash of a fountain, then few deep-water aquatics, except the rather vulgar yellow pondlily (*Nuphar lutea*), will prosper.

Marginal aquatics are widely used for formal arrangements, especially reeds and rushes, although strong foliage plants like cannas and pontederia are excellent for focal plantings. All aquatic plants are best grown in planting baskets. Not only is this practical and functional but it ensures that the plants remain precisely where they should and do not "wander off" and spoil the carefully contrived visual effect.

Below: There is no reason why a formal pool cannot be heavily planted if the distinct outlines of the feature remain clearly visible. The use of architectural plants with formal foliage can greatly enhance the overall appearance of the feature.

Right: Formality on a grand scale. The pool, arbor, and lawned areas are all beautifully in proportion with one another. Although the pool has clearly been placed to provide a reflection of the building, the water surface is not unduly cluttered by the clumps of water lilies. The marginal plants in each corner of the pool both add to the formality and soften the paved edges.

self-contained formal features

Water as a permanent structural feature in the garden is important, but if this is impractical and additional small bodies of water would better enhance the scene, then troughs, tubs, and containers can be used in a formal style. There is a danger that these elements could have a fragmented or punctuated effect in a formal garden. However, if suitable vessels are chosen, such as galvanized or lead tanks and cisterns, pleasing effects can be achieved that sit well in a formal garden.

It is possible to use tubs and half-barrels, especially in small intimate areas, and particularly when they are devoid of plants and perhaps converted to a pebble fountain or bubbler. However, in the wider expanse of a garden, tubs and half-barrels can seem rather out of place unless they are constructed of modern metals or plastics. In such circumstances they can be very startling and eye-catching, especially when used with a fogging device or simple single jet fountain.

Whatever self-contained feature is used, the gardener must realize that there will be greater maintenance implications than with a pool. The body of water is so small and the temperature changes likely to be so great that algal blooms will be a regular and unsightly occurrence, so the use of algaecides and the regular topping off and changing of the water are likely to be required. Developing a natural aquatic eco-balance is not feasible in such cases.

Right: This combination of tubs and a hand pump make a very effective self-contained water feature. It is served by a submersible pump in the lower barrel.

Left: Self-contained water features come in a wide range of configurations. This elegant formal fountain is operated by a submersible pump in a reservoir. It is important to appreciate the amount of water loss that such a feature will experience, both from evaporation and from water splash. It will need to be topped off on a regular basis.

Above: The traditional wall fountain or gargoyle is ideal in confined spaces and particularly effective in the courtyard garden where the sound of falling water will be magnified by the surrounding walls. The submersible pump that operates the fountain is situated in the large trough. A feature like this can either stand alone or be tastefully planted for a less formal effect.

basic principles

When establishing a pond, it is important to consider the site very carefully. Certain factors will affect the pond visually and by nature are subjective, but others will affect the way the pond functions, and they should be carefully considered.

The most important factor is sunlight. A pond must be positioned in full uninterrupted sunlight if the plants and fish are to prosper. Sunlight is important for the plants, because none of the popularly grown varieties of aquatics are tolerant of shade. Sunlight is equally important for a formal pool consisting of just open water and no plants, because it is the play of light with its varied reflections upon the water that gives the pool its appeal. If the pond is being constructed during the winter, observe nearby deciduous trees, because these may cast shadows in unexpected areas during the summer when they are in full leaf.

The falling leaves from trees can be a nuisance during the autumn, so overhanging branches must be avoided. Unfortunately, these are not the only contributor to leaf-fall problems within the pond: It is an undisputed fact that once a water feature is established, all leaves in the neighborhood blow around and congregate there. Wind-blown leaves can be readily excluded by constructing a low temporary fence around the pond at leaf fall.

Many trees have invasive roots, those of willows and poplar being particularly disruptive. When in close proximity to a pond, they can cause heaving and fracturing of the liner. Cherry and plum trees are the host of water lily aphids during the winter months, and they should be kept at arm's length, and willows have foliage that is highly toxic to fish.

The site for a pond must also be well drained. Ironically, a permanently wet area may not be a good position for a

MAKING THE POOL SAFE

1 Using a drill with a masonry bit, drill holes into the paved pool surround at regular intervals. Ideally the holes should be equidistant from the edges of each slab.

There are no easy solutions to making the pool safe for small children. The use of a removable wire grille is practical and causes the least disruption.

2 Insert a wall plug in each hole, hammering it home firmly. This should be matched to a large eyelet, which can be screwed and unscrewed as necessary.

3 The metal grille is firmly secured with a padlock through the eyelet and grille. Oil the padlocks regularly to prevent them from corroding and becoming difficult to undo.

Right: *All the conditions for a successful garden pond are embodied here. A level site in full sun has been chosen well away from shading buildings and overhanging trees. The pool is far enough from the house to avoid any underground utilities in the vicinity. The plants are prospering, an indication that they were planted at the proper depths. The water is clear, and so a naturally balanced ecosystem has been achieved.*

pond because the pressure of a high water table can dislodge a preformed structure, literally forcing it out of the soil, and also cause the liner to balloon.

Safety is an important consideration when there are children around. During construction, arrange to have a temporary fence (for example, removable screening or netting) installed to cover the pond, including securing eyelets to edging stones for fastening netting or a wire frame. Then the fencing can be taken away when you want to enjoy the pool in all its uncluttered glory.

Finally the cost implications must be carefully assessed. It may not be possible to do everything at once, but careful planning from the outset is extremely helpful in ensuring that additions, such as a bog garden or a filter, can be added when sufficient funds become available, without appearing as afterthoughts.

CHECK LIST

- Choose as level a site as possible.
- Ensure that the site is not waterlogged. Drain if necessary. Choose an open sunny site.
- Check the position of underground utilities, such as gas and water, before starting to dig; make sure that an electrical supply is available nearby if moving water is considered.
- Avoid overhanging trees.
- Distance the pool from disruptive rooted trees, like poplar and willow. Avoid cherry trees, the overwintering host of water lily aphids. Also avoid willows because their leaves are toxic to fish.
- Make arrangements to dispose of excavated soil.
- Make sure deep-water and marginal aquatics are planted at suitable depths within the water.
- Make any preparations necessary to ensure that safety measures can be made to keep children safe.
- Plan the whole concept carefully from the outset.

options and materials

There are many options for construction with a formal pool. Traditionally concrete was preferred, but this has now been largely superseded by other materials. Concrete can still be used effectively, but it is difficult for home gardeners to use unless they are builders by profession. It is heavy, often requires elaborate shuttering, and is laborious to mix. The end result is pleasing, but it then requires special treatment if fish are to be introduced, because the free lime escaping into the water is harmful to them.

Many formal preformed pools are available commercially, and with careful selection these are excellent choices. Make sure that the marginal shelves are sufficiently deep to accommodate a planting basket and that the edges are manufactured in such a manner that they can easily be disguised by paving or decking. Preformed pools are made from many different materials, those manufactured from vacuum-formed plastic being the least appealing and most difficult to install, although unquestionably the cheapest. The best are manufactured from a composite plastic material or fiberglass.

Pool liners are the easiest to install and can be used to produce wonderful results. LDPE (low-density polyethelene) and butyl rubber liners are the most durable and unquestionably the best to use for a permanent construction. Their great advantage is they can be used to produce a pool of almost any size or configuration with little excavation because they conform to the shape of the hole dug. Preformed pools require more digging to be done!

Below: A preformed pool should offer various depths to suit the requirements of aquatic plants and fish. The marginal shelves here are self-contained and conveniently divided so that planting can take place directly onto them.

Right: A pool liner enables any shape or size of pool to be constructed. A wide range of materials is available, from PVC to rubber composition. The expensive rubber types are the most durable, although the low-density polyethelene types are an excellent value.

CONCRETE POOL CONSTRUCTION

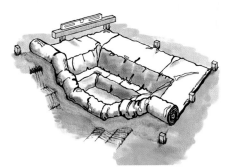

1 *Excavate a hole 6 inches (15 cm) larger than the finished pool to allow for the thickness of concrete. Line this with polythene.*

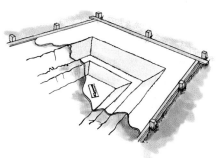

2 *Make a wood frame to define the excavation. Working from the center, spread the concrete out to a depth of 4 inches (10 cm).*

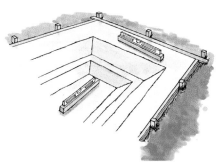

3 *Check your levels in all directions. Make sure the concrete is reasonably smooth, and then add a layer of reinforced wire mesh.*

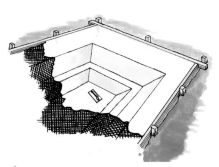

4 *Press the reinforced wire mesh into the wet concrete. Cover with a 2-inch (5-cm) layer of concrete, and make a smooth finish.*

5 *Remove the wood frame, and cover the concrete with damp sacking or similar material and water to prevent cracking.*

6 *Once the concrete has dried out, apply a sealant to prevent free lime from escaping. Alternatively use a plastic pond paint.*

CALCULATING POOL CAPACITY

Rectangular Pools

• Multiply length by width by depth (in meters) to obtain volume in cubic meters. Multiply this by 1,000 to give the capacity in liters.

• Multiply length by width by depth (in feet) to obtain volume in cubic feet. Multiply this by 6.23 to give capacity in imperial gallons.

Circular Pools

• Multiply depth in meters by the square of the radius (r^2) in meters x π (3.1416) x 1,000 to give capacity in liters.

• Multiply depth in feet by the square of the radius (r^2) in feet x π (3.1416) x 6.23 to give approximate capacity in imperial gallons.

Facts and Figures

• One imperial gallon of water occupies 0.16 cubic feet and weighs 10 pounds.

• One U.S. gallon is equivalent to 0.83268 imperial gallons and weighs 8.3 pounds.

• One cubic foot of water is equivalent to 6.23 imperial gallons or 28.3 liters and weighs 62.32 pounds.

• One imperial gallon equals 160 fluid ounces or 4.546 liters.

• One liter equals 1.76 imperial pints or 0.22 imperial gallons or 35.196 fluid ounces.

• One liter equals 0.264 U.S. gallons.

pumps and filters

Modern submersible pumps have ensured that everyone has the opportunity to introduce moving water into the garden without the need for major engineering work. They are available in a wide range of shapes and sizes and can create everything from a gentle trickle to a thundering foamy spray. Even when large volumes of water have to be moved, a modest submersible pump can be found to do the job. The days of the surface pump housed in a specially built brick chamber are over, except for major water features.

In the formal pool featuring moving water, it is quite common that there will be no plant life nor a semblance of an ecosystem. This results in a number of problems, such as the presence of free-floating unicellular algae, which turn the water green, and the swirling around of aquatic dust and debris. A submersible pump will take some of the larger particles out as the water passes through its simple filter sponge, but for other debris to be removed and water clarity to be achieved, it is necessary to attach a filter system.

There are many filter systems that can be used. They fall into three main categories: the kind that physically separates out particles and debris, the biological kind in which colonies of bacteria that convert harmful substances in the water to harmless ones grow, and the ultraviolet kind, which employs an ultraviolet (UV) lamp to kill off algae and other living organisms that discolor the water. Filters that combine these roles are also available. They can either be situated within the pool or as an external filter sited in a chamber outside the water feature.

INSIDE A PUMP AND FILTER

1 *The component parts of a submersible pump are easily separated for cleaning. The unit on the right is the motor.*

2 *The impeller assembly, which moves the water, is simply connected to the pump body with a small wrench.*

3 *The motor section locks onto the impeller assembly. Modern motors are surprisingly small and very powerful.*

4 *The filter assembly clips on to the pump unit. This physically traps debris and algae and is regularly removed for cleaning.*

5 *This in-pond filter combines both physical and biological filtration systems. The parts can easily be separated for cleaning.*

6 *The filter cartridge is inserted into the filter chamber. The filter sponge can be rinsed.*

7 *The core containing a filter medium is fitted into the cover.*

8 *The filter is connected to a submersible pump and placed alongside it on a plinth or preferably the pond floor. The pump draws water through the filter, and the dirt and debris are strained out.*

An ultraviolet (UV) filter that destroys algae as they pass through it. The UV light kills the algae, which then clump together and can be removed by mechanical filtration.

THE RIGHT PUMP SIZE

When buying a pump, it is important that you calculate the flow rate that you need to achieve—this depends on the size of the pool and the number of features that you want the pump to service. For a pump to run more than one feature, you will need to make certain allowances in your calculations to establish the flow rate that your chosen pump must achieve.

Here are some guidelines to help calculate flow requirements:
- A filter requires half the volume of the pond pumped through it every hour.
- A waterfall needs 360 gallons (approx. 1,385 liters) per hour for every 6 inches (15 cm) of waterfall width required.
- A fountain or ornament requires an extra 30 percent flow.
- An extra 25 percent flow should be added for loss of flow through pipework.

The following two examples show typical setups for which the correct pump must be selected.

Features wanted	Flow calculation	Flow required
9 inches (22.5 cm) wide waterfall	(9/6) x 360	= 540 gallons/hr
A fountain	540 x 30%	= 162 gallons/hr
Allow for pipework	(540 + 162) x 25%	= 176 gallons/hr
	Total flow rate needed	= 878 gallons/hr

Features wanted	Flow calculation	Flow required
Filter for 594-gallon pond	594/2	= 297 gallons/hr
An ornament	297 x 30%	= 89 gallons/hr
Allow for pipework	(297 + 89) x 25%	= 97 gallons/hr
	Total flow rate needed	= 483 gallons/hr

When selecting the appropriate pump, you must also make allowance for the maximum head required—that is, the maximum height to which the water has to be pumped above the pond surface. The effective flow rate of a pump will drop off the higher it has to pump water above the pool surface. Ask for advice in your local aquatic or garden center to ensure that the pump you select will be able to provide the required flow at the maximum operational head.

Left: *A water feature with constantly moving water, especially where there are no aquatic plants present and the surrounding hard landscape is likely to be dusty, creates a real challenge. In such situations, a powerful pump and a filter that physically removes debris from the water is vital to ensure good water quality.*

marking out the site

Having selected a suitable site, the first task is to accurately mark out the position of the pool. For a liner pool, this can be done with a series of strings, pegs, and simple mathematical formulas, which most of us learned at school. When using a liner, it is important to be very accurate with the size and profile of the pool, especially if the liner is prepurchased. Experienced water gardeners typically excavate first and then measure accurately to ensure that they have accounted for everything in the excavation when calculating the length of liner to be bought.

Apart from ensuring accuracy of form, it is important to get the pool level. Even a small deviation can cause both water spillage on one side and exposure of the inner pool-side on the other. Position a mean level peg, and then work from this with a board and level, ensuring that the whole area is accurately assessed. Soil can then be redistributed according to the various levels indicated by the pegs. When installing a liner, it is preferable to take the lowest point in the leveling process and to transfer the mean level peg to that position. Although it is possible to raise levels by filling with soil, when using a liner it is preferable to excavate so that the soil remains solid and undisturbed.

With a preformed pool, this is not so critical, but accurate leveling is just as vital. Although some suggest that accurate excavation to accommodate the shelves of a preformed pool is possible, it is generally preferable to dig a hole that is the maximum length, breadth, and depth of the pool and to position it within that hole. Backfilling any voids in the soil once the preformed pool is in place is usually easiest with pea gravel. This leaves a considerable amount of soil to dispose of around the garden. If there is too much to redistribute, then it is best to take it away rather than create a clay mound with a few added stones and optimistically call it a rock garden.

MARKING OUT AN OVAL

1 *Knock in pegs at both ends, and one in the center. Add two more at two-thirds the distance between the center and end pegs.*

2 *Tie a length of string around four of the pegs—not all five. This establishes the correct length for the marker.*

3 *Now loop this length of string around the three inner pegs, and take up the slack with a sharp piece of bamboo cane.*

4 *Making sure that the string is held taut, score a line in the turf with the bamboo moving in a curve around the center peg.*

5 *As you move around toward the end peg, the cane will naturally inscribe an oval shape on the ground.*

6 *To make the outline clear, sprinkle sand freely along it.*

MARKING A CIRCLE

1 *Place a peg in the center of the intended circle. Attach a string, and use a second cane to inscribe the circumference.*

2 *Use sand to distinguish the score mark clearly in the turf. It also gives a good impression of how the finished pool will fit into the garden plan.*

Left: This formal arrangement shows clearly the skills of the mathematician and surveyor and is something to which the formal water gardener may wish to aspire. If the component parts are tackled separately, using simple marking-out techniques, in reality such intricate layouts are not as difficult to create as they may at first appear.

A right angle can be created by marking out a triangle using Pythagoras's 3-4-5 system of measurement.

ESTABLISHING LEVELS

1 *You must establish the levels of the ground where the pool is to be dug. Set a datum peg to the desired level, and use more pegs and a spirit level to establish the horizontal.*

2 *Measure the distance to the ground of your first datum peg. This is the level at which you want all the edges of the pool to sit when it has been excavated.*

3 *Now transfer this measurement to the other pegs in all directions across the site. This shows where the soil needs cutting away or filling up to establish a flat surround.*

installing an external filter

External filters permit the regular treatment of pond water and produce excellent results. Most extract solid debris, and also pass the water through bioblocks or similar material where helpful aerobic bacteria convert toxic ammonia into nitrites and ultimately nitrates. If a carbon-impregnated pad is included in the outflow, then organic wastes can be completely eliminated from the water.

External filters can be positioned on the surface of the ground next to the pool and discreetly hidden by vegetation. However, it is neater to sink them into the ground, in a purpose-built chamber near the summit of a waterfall. It is wise to create a firm base by using a paving slab or bricks so that the filter box is level in its chamber.

Once the filter box has been positioned, the lid can be replaced and the hole backfilled, provided the box is not disturbed. If a UV filter is needed to kill algae in the water, the filter can be accommodated next to the main filter box; however, it is then necessary to run the filter feed hose into the pool. If the filter is situated close to the top of a waterfall, it is best to conceal the hose at the base of the waterfall.

The biofilter and UV filter can then be connected and the pump attached to the filter feed hose. Once the pump is turned on, the filtration process begins. It will take four to six weeks in warm weather before the biological part of the filter establishes sufficient beneficial bacteria to break down the harmful toxins in the water and the pond chemistry starts to improve.

INSTALLING AN EXTERNAL FILTER

1 *First excavate the area where you want to sink the filter chamber into the ground.*

2 *Use a paving slab or a layer of bricks to provide a firm and level base for the filter.*

3 *Put the filter chamber in position. Make sure it is level and secure before backfilling.*

4 *Replace the lid, and backfill around the sides, using either soil or fine pea gravel.*

5 *If the filter has a UV option, attach this close to the main filter chamber so it is easily accessible when needed.*

6 *With the UV attachment in place, run the filter feed hose into the pool. When the filter is positioned close to a waterfall as is illustrated here, it is easiest to conceal the hose in the rocks at the base of the waterfall.*

7 *The pump is then attached to the filter. Make sure that the pump is powerful enough to effectively operate the filter.*

8 *Run the pump to make sure that it works properly. The biological filter will take several weeks to become fully effective.*

Above: *Excavations are not always necessary to successfully accommodate a filter. Rather than concealing it in the ground, the filter in this delightful formal arrangement is disguised by lush vegetation.*

9 *It is a good idea to plant vegetation around the filter that will grow up and hide it from view. Once the filter is working efficiently, water clarity in the pool can almost be assured.*

making a round lined pool

A circular pool is slightly more difficult to construct using a liner than one that is square or oblong, largely because it is more complicated to make the necessary folds of the liner so that they are unobtrusive. However, in every other respect, it follows the methods used for the less-complex liner constructions of square formal ponds.

Marking out is achieved simply by using the two stakes and string method—a string the length of the radius of the pool is attached to a central stake on one end and a sharpened stake on the other. The sharpened one scores out the position of the pool edge as it is scribed around the central peg in a circle. A trickle of sand can be used to delineate the outline more clearly if necessary. The depth and shelving arrangements should then be calculated and a quantity of liner purchased based on the maximum length and breadth of the finished pool (measurements that are, of course, identical for a circular pool) plus twice the maximum depth.

The site of the excavation must be made level, or water will spill from the pool at one point and liner will be exposed at the opposite side. It is much simpler to prepare for this before digging begins than to try to rectify it when the liner has been laid and water added. The excavation should also ideally be created in undisturbed soil so that the soil does not move around. Thus it is always preferable when leveling the site to reduce a higher area rather than to add soil to a lower area.

The excavation is made to precisely the dimensions of the intended final pool, any sharp stones or other debris being carefully removed and protective pool underlay fabric installed. Damp bricklayers' sand can also be used to form a protective cushion, but this is not so useful where there are significantly steep sides to cater for.

EXCAVATING A ROUND POOL

1 *Mark out a circle on the ground using two pegs and a piece of string that is the length of the radius of the finished pool.*

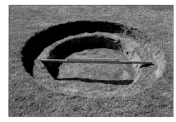

2 *Remove the turf to produce the outline of the pool. Use a sharp spade or a turfing iron to make a neat job of the excavation.*

3 *It is important that the excavation is level, because this will provide the pool profile. Chec the ground with a board and level regularly.*

4 *Make sure that the marginal shelves are level across the excavation in each direction and of the correct depth.*

5 *Scour the excavation, and remove any sharp stones, twigs, or other objects that could pierce the liner under the weight of water.*

6 *As an added precaution to guard against puncture, a layer of sand can be spread over the base of the excavation and the shelves.*

Above: *A beautiful pool can be created easily and economically with a liner. Once established, it has a look of permanence usually associated with a concrete construction.*

7 *The completed excavation is carefully lined with pond liner underlay. Water it to help it conform to the shape of the hole.*

8 *The pool liner is placed as accurately as possible within the hole. Large regular folds are then made to eliminate creases.*

9 *Water is added. As the water rises, the folds can be adjusted and any small creases or wrinkles in the liner smoothed out.*

The liner should be spread out to warm in the summer sun before being introduced to the excavated hole. This makes it much more malleable and eases the problem of making neat folds when the time comes to do this. Water is then added, and the liner begins to stretch to accommodate itself to the excavation. At this stage, creases should be smoothed away as far as possible and the folds in the liner made to help it conform to the shape of the hole. Once the water level has reached the top, the liner edge can be trimmed so that it can be disguised beneath paving or whatever edging is intended.

The method by which a preformed pool is installed is not dissimilar, except that the excavation should be larger and space should be left around the entire pool for backfilling. Pools made from vacuum-formed plastic have little rigidity, so water must be added as backfilling takes place, otherwise the soft plastic walls of the pool will buckle inward. Although it has always been traditional to backfill with soil from the excavation site, much better results are achieved with the use of pea gravel, which flows easily between the sides of the pool and the soil. This avoids creating any voids or air pockets, a common problem if lumpy, uncompromising clay soil from the excavation is used.

As with a lined pool, a preformed pool should be installed with the edges level to avoid water spillage. The level should be checked regularly while backfilling because a preformed pool will move as the pea gravel flows around. Always allow play of about 1 inch (2.5 cm) for the pool to rise within the excavation as backfilling takes place.

Above: *This circular pool is neatly edged with paving. The use of specially manufactured paving slabs that are deliberately curved makes a neat circular construction such as this relatively straightforward to build.*

EDGING THE POOL

1 *Paving slabs provide the best formal edging. Allow a small overhang to produce a neat edge, and remove any surplus liner.*

2 *Excavate the area beneath the slab and liner, and fill back to ground level with mortar. Poolside paving must be secure.*

3 *Lay the slabs, and make sure that they are level in every direction. Point the gaps between them evenly with mortar.*

Right: Paving is a neat method of finishing the edge of a circular pool, but it can also be an integral part of the garden scene. Here the extensive paved areas add much to the beauty of the pool, extending its influence into the surrounding garden landscape. They also provide safe and ready access for the enjoyment of the pool, the adjacent areas also being of sufficient size to permit recreation and relaxation at the waterside. The planting in and around the margins of the pool helps to soften its contours.

making a raised pool

There are many options for building a raised pool, ranging from a standard brick or stone wall construction to a timber sleeper arrangement. It is possible to use an existing watertight vessel, such as a header tank, and build around it, or the feature may be created from scratch. For the inventive gardener, the latter option is usually preferred, for then the pool can be exactly what is required, rather than the inevitable compromise offered by a container disguised by a surrounding wall.

As with pools that are sunk in the ground, it is important to have a level base from which to work with a raised pool. Remember that the underlying level of the ground is transferred upward with a raised pool, and the problems of spillage and liner exposure are potentially the same.

Of all the construction materials that are available, properly preserved timber is the most versatile and also the most resistant to severe winter weather. In areas where hard or prolonged frosts are common, a brick construction can suffer badly from fracturing, stemming either from the expansion of the ice in freezing conditions or the shaling of the surface of the bricks (unless engineering bricks are used). Timber is a warmer material visually and also has sufficient flexibility in it to withstand any movement within the pool that the freezing of water can cause.

Installing a liner is very easy in a timber pool, because it can be readily secured to the internal wooden walls using a narrow batten to trap the liner, which is then secured with roofing nails.

MAKING A RAISED TIMBER POOL

1 *Place the sleeper timbers in a square arrangement. Make sure that each one overlaps the junction between the timbers below it.*

2 *Secure the timbers in place with strong metal strips or ties. Use self-tapping screws and an electric screwdriver.*

3 *Measure the pool liner and fit it accurately into the structure, making bold folds in the corners to minimize creasing.*

4 *Using a staple gun, secure the liner to the wooden structure. Position the staples near the top edge of the liner. The timber batten will cover them.*

5 *Align the timber batten with the top edge of the timber structure so as to trap the liner in place. Secure it with roofing nails.*

6 *Create a marginal planting pocket by putting a square of liner underlay in a corner, and build a boxlike structure with loose bricks.*

7 *Once the container area has been completed, add good garden soil or aquatic planting compost. Plant into this, and top-dress with pea gravel.*

8 *The completed pool. Architectural plants like bulrush and pickerel have been used to add a strong vertical note to the feature.*

Right: *A raised pool makes a strong statement in this garden.*

Goldfish and shubunkins bring the pool to life and control insect pests.

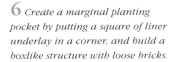

installing a formal patio pool

There are many opportunities for creating a small water feature on a patio. It is mostly undesirable to excavate a pool in such a position, because the soil is unlikely to be compacted and stable, and that is a prerequisite when using a liner. It is more likely that a layer of small rocks will need to be removed before soil level is reached. Apart from such vagaries of construction, which need not dissuade the enthusiast from creating such a pool if it is deemed an essential part of the garden's design, a sunken pool in a patio will gather all sorts of leaves and debris that blow into it. A raised pool not only alleviates these practical problems but offers the gardener the opportunity to enjoy the beauty of the plants and activities of the fish closer to hand.

Raised pools available to the home gardener are generally of simple construction, but they are very effective. Most are round or octagonal, although some are square, and either consist of a rigid container around which an outer decorative surround is built or are of a modular construction, usually of timber, which is lined with a pool liner that is secured internally with wooden battens or carpet strip. Although most constructions depend on a conventional lining, there are now some in which the pool liner is preformed and welded into a shape that drops into the structure where it fits exactly, without any need for folds or tucks.

As with a pool that is excavated in the ground, the raised pool demands a level surface. In kit form, the modern raised patio pool is of very straightforward construction and is one of the most satisfactory formal water features when constraints of space demand a small-scale construction for the terrace or patio.

MAKING A SELF-BUILD PATIO POOL

1 *The preformed timber sections are already treated with a preservative, but they are bland and uninteresting. Garden stains or wood paints help brighten their appearance.*

2 *Small metal fasteners are screwed into the main bearers, both at the top and the bottom. These provide the structure with rigidity. It is important that they are accurately installed.*

Above: *Apart from self-assembly patio pools, many other small-scale do-it-yourself water features are available. This bubbling pot fountain sits on top of a water reservoir hidden beneath the cobbles.*

3 *When most of the sections have been screwed together, the tub that forms the pool is slid into the prepared framework. The final fixings are then made.*

4 *Once the whole pool structure is complete, it can be positioned. It is important to have a level situation, such as a terrace, on which to site it permanently.*

5 *Fill the pool with water. It looks best if the final level in such a pool is established just a couple of centimeters beneath the overhang of the top surround.*

6 *If a pump is to be installed, create a small level plinth with a few loose housebricks. The depth is determined by the length of the fountain attachment.*

7 *Position the pump centrally, and make sure that the top of the fountain nozzle is just above the water surface. Take care to hide the electrical cable as neatly as possible.*

8 *Switch the pump on and adjust the spray height to suit the space available. Water splash and the height of the jet in relation to its surroundings should be considered.*

edging with stone and brick

The edge of the formal pond is usually easier to deal with than that of the informal pool because it has a definite line of hard landscaping to help delineate the formal shape of the pool. Stone, paving, and bricks can all play a part in providing a suitable edge; however, such an edging is not only ornamental but functional as well, which is why it must be safe to walk on at any point. Formal pools by their very nature are uncluttered and when edged with paving or bricks they invite the visitor to dwell at the edge.

There are a wide range of hard landscape edging materials that can be used, but paving stones are the most popular. These are available in various colors, sizes, and finishes. From a visual viewpoint it is important to select a size that rests easily with the surface area of the pool. Large paving stones around a small pool rarely provide a pleasing arrangement, just as small ones in a single row around a large pool do little to enhance it. However, several rows of smaller pavers in a patterned arrangement can be visually satisfying.

Bricks and paving stones must all be fixed securely on a generous mortar bed. The mortar should not go right to the water's edge because spillage into the pool results in the release of harmful free lime, and the pond will need to be emptied and cleaned before stocking can take place. However, the mortar should be sufficient to secure the bricks or paving stones, which ideally should protrude just over the edge of the pool. This effect not only creates a much neater finish than when the stones are aligned directly with the wall of the pool, but in a lined pool it also gives some measure of protection to the liner from the bleaching effect of the sun beating down on it above the waterline.

MAKING A STONE PAVED EDGE

1 *Mark the edge of the pool with an edger. This should correspond with the outer edge of the paving stone when in its final position.*

2 *Remove a strip of turf or the soil up to the back edge. Allow a retaining lip of undisturbed soil to remain next to the water's edge.*

3 *Pull the liner and pool underlay tightly over the lip and back over the excavation and secure it in position in readiness for the mortar.*

4 *Fill the excavated area with mortar. Extend this up to the lip, but not over it. The lip will prevent mortar spillage into the pond.*

5 *Carefully position the slabs. Curved slabs fit a round pool most easily, but you can create an attractive feature with oblong ones.*

6 *Work around the circumference of the pool, firming each slab in place as you go. Check the levels regularly. Poolside paving must be level.*

Above: *A circular pool beautifully edged with paving slabs. Here pebbles have been set in concrete in a ring outside the slabs for wholly decorative effect. The planting softens the outer reaches of the feature.*

7 *Put a small piece of card beneath the gap at the poolside to prevent mortar spillage.*

8 *Put mortar between the paving slabs and add selected pebbles for decorative effect.*

9 *Once the mortar has dried out, remove the card shuttering from beneath the slabs.*

edging with decking and timber

Today, garden decking comes in all shapes and forms. It is particularly useful and appropriate at the poolside. Not only can it be effectively used as an edging material, but with a little imagination it can also be used as a viewing or sitting place, or with larger pools as a small jetty or causeway. For the small formal pool, decking is commonly used to integrate the edge of the water feature with the surrounding garden. This can also be simply achieved with plain timber that has been pressure-treated with a preservative.

Decking boards come in various designs, not only as single straight boards but also in preconstructed patterns. They are normally heavily grooved, and they are treated with a preservative which—even when in contact with the pool water—is harmless to plants and fish. The patterned shapes can be used visually rather like paving slabs, but of course they must be fixed securely to timber supports. Apart from producing a straight formal edge, timber structures can also be used to project over a formal pool, to make a convenient spot for sitting or viewing the fish.

A solid timber base is needed to secure decking as an edge. During construction of a liner pool, large timbers or sleepers may be incorporated behind the liner and bedded into the surrounding soil. This method is useful because the timbers provide both a surface to which the liner can be secured and a support to which decking or a plain timber edge can be screwed or fastened.

Left: Decking is very important in providing a sitting area for dining and recreation. In most water gardens it also helps to disguise the pool edge. Here timber is used freely as a unifying factor throughout the whole garden design. All timber edging should be pretreated with a wood preservative. The wide variety of garden paints and stains now available can be brought into play to add a little visual zest to the garden scene.

EDGING WITH TIMBER

1 *Measure accurately the lengths of timber that are required to form the edge. Joints are undesirable, except in the corners.*

2 *Cut the timbers to length, taking care to ensure a straight edge. Sand the cut edges to make them completely smooth.*

3 *When positioning the boards, allow a small gap between them for movement in the timber, and screw them down securely.*

4 *The color of the timber can be altered with a garden paint or decking stain.*

Above: *The finished edge. This is very durable and goes well with plants both inside and outside the pool.*

Above: *An interesting edge created by the extension of decking as an overhang. It is important that, when used this way, all the timbers are firmly secured. Remember that visitors may stand right at the edge, so any extension must be sturdy.*

introducing movement and lights

A formal pool lends itself beautifully to the use of moving water and carefully placed lighting. In many cases, the two are complementary. Indeed it is quite possible to purchase a pump to produce a fountain with an attachment that provides uplighting. In the most sophisticated form, colored lenses are used to create different light colors and patterns. For those who desire the latest sophistication, it is even possible to introduce a submersible pump with a fountain and lighting attachment that will produce dancing water and light patterns that are linked to a music system and synchronized with the sound.

For most gardeners, a simple submersible pump is adequate. Simplicity is key to creating a successful moving water feature in a formal setting. A single jet or plume of water is just as effective as complex waterworks – if not more so. Likewise with lighting, simple white light is difficult to surpass, and it is often easier for the home gardener to create pleasing effects with it than with the multicolored lights that are available.

The placement of a fountain is almost solely a matter of aesthetics. Modern submersible pumps are simple to introduce to a pool; the pump is positioned in the pool on a plinth or directly on the pool floor and connected to the power. A similar process is used with lights. Provided specially manufactured garden lighting is used, it is safe and simple to install, either around the pond or, where appropriate, beneath the water. Make sure that the lights are concentrated on a focal point, whether it be a fountain or plant. General diffuse lighting without a focus of attention is a wasted opportunity.

WARNING Electricity and water make a dangerous combination. Make sure that any electrical device running off mains power is protected by a residual current device (RCD) or circuit breaker that will cut off the supply instantly in the event of a short circuit.

BUILDING A FOUNTAIN PLINTH

1 *When introducing a fountain to a pool, it is usually necessary to create a plinth or other level support. When the pool is lined, lay a piece of pool underlay on which to position a paving slab. Make sure that the slab is level.*

2 *Place bricks on the paving slab. The number that are required will depend on the depth of the pool and the length of the fountain spray attachment. If more than one row of bricks is required, arrange them alternately.*

3 *A paving slab is placed on the top of the bricks. Make sure that this is secure and level. The pump can then be put in position. Try to lead the electrical cable out of the pool in the most discreet manner possible. Yards and yards of trailing flex is unsightly.*

4 *Attach the fountain spray unit to the pump. The head of the unit will need to be just above the final surface level of the water for the best spray effect.*

Above: *Apart from conventional spray heads, there are myriad decorative spray assemblies. Here a large water lily ornament serves as the fountain head.*

Right: *A classic fountain throwing water into the air in well-defined sprays of droplets. The height will need periodic adjusting according to wind conditions.*

pond chemistry

The chemistry of pond water is a subject often treated with mystery and reverence. In reality, if plant and fish populations are in harmony, the chances of it being seriously awry are remote. Even with a small pool where there is considerable vulnerability, the instances of pond chemistry being a cause for major concern are uncommon. A pool is much more resilient than an aquarium, where water chemistry is a major daily concern.

The main questions the pond owner needs to address are ones of nitrate level and acidity or alkalinity. Both can be tested using a simple kit that is available from most garden centers. Nitrate levels are rarely a problem if fertilizer residues from the garden do not seep into the pool and fish stock levels are maintained at a sensible level. Problems do sometimes occur with an over-population of fish, because ammonia is produced from fish waste decomposing in the water. When nitrate levels are unacceptably high, the usual remedy is to clean and wash out the pool thoroughly and, if the quantity of fish is believed to be a contributing factor, to reduce the number of fish.

Acidity and alkalinity are not usually troublesome unless in the extreme. Again a simple pond pH test kit can be used to determine the pH, but indicators such as the condition of snail shells are almost as reliable. In acid water, the shells become pitted, whereas in alkaline water they are fine and smooth. Plants can be another useful indicator of water chemistry. Water soldiers, *Stratiotes aloides*, emerge above the surface in alkaline conditions as the true floaters that they are, but under acid conditions they become suspended midway beneath the water. When water becomes too acid or alkaline, the only safe way of correcting the problem is to empty the pool and refill it with fresh water.

THE NITROGEN CYCLE

Fish naturally excrete waste, which falls to the bottom of the pond and decomposes. This increases the amount of ammonia, the toxicity of which rises with the water temperature. Under natural conditions, bacteria break down the ammonia into nitrites, which are still harmful to fish. Other bacteria then convert nitrites into relatively harmless nitrates, which are taken up by the plants. In a heavily populated pond, or where fish are overfed, there are often insufficient bacteria to cope with the quantity of ammonia and nitrites in the water. The introduction of a filter where the beneficial bacteria prosper and troublesome debris is captured helps to overcome the likelihood of nitrite or ammonia toxicity.

Right: A beautifully clear pond where the water chemistry is evidently perfect. The plants are flourishing, and it is possible to see right through the water to the stones on the floor of the pool.

TESTING POND WATER

Above: Periodic testing for nitrate levels is important, especially if there are many fish in the pond.

Left: pH test kits indicate the acidity or alkalinity of the water. Unless there are extremes either way, the majority of aquatic plants and ornamental fish will be quite content.

Right: Cottongrass, Eriophorum angustifolium, *is a plant that is adversely affected by alkaline conditions. To prosper, it must have acid water conditions.*

plants for formal features

There are an enormous number of aquatic plants that can be used effectively in formal ponds. These are mainly plants that give the features a particular theme or ambience, although those that are purely practical should not be overlooked. Submerged plants can make an important contribution to the well-being of the ecology of the smaller pool, although visually they are of no significance. Choose species that rarely punctuate the water surface; those like *Lagarosiphon major* and *Elodea canadensis* are preferable when the glassy mirror-like stillness of the pool is important. Lovely though they are, free-flowering submerged plants that raise their blossoms above the water, such as the water crowfoot (*Ranunculus aquatilis*) and water violet (*Hottonia palustris*), can so easily detract from the desired effect.

Water lilies are excellent plants for creating surface interest. These root into baskets in the lower reaches of the pool and then push up their floating leaves and blossoms. All are excellent, but be sure to choose varieties that are suitable for the depth of water in the pool. If the water is too deep they will struggle and leaf sparsely, but conversely if too shallow they will climb out of the water in an unruly lump.

It is the marginal plants that set off formal water features. Architectural plants of easygoing disposition like *Schoenoplectus lacustris* and its variegated-leafed cousin, the zebra rush, can be used to add a vertical note to the feature. The pickerel (*Pontederia cordata*) is a stately foliage plant and lovely when in flower, as are the recently introduced aquatic cannas known as 'Longwood Hybrids'.

CROSS-SECTION OF A POND SHOWING PLANTING DEPTHS

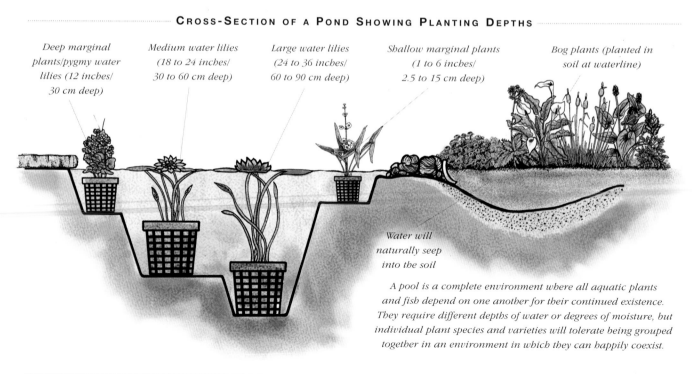

Deep marginal plants/pygmy water lilies (12 inches/ 30 cm deep)

Medium water lilies (18 to 24 inches/ 30 to 60 cm deep)

Large water lilies (24 to 36 inches/ 60 to 90 cm deep)

Shallow marginal plants (1 to 6 inches/ 2.5 to 15 cm deep)

Bog plants (planted in soil at waterline)

Water will naturally seep into the soil

A pool is a complete environment where all aquatic plants and fish depend on one another for their continued existence. They require different depths of water or degrees of moisture, but individual plant species and varieties will tolerate being grouped together in an environment in which they can happily coexist.

RECOMMENDED PLANT LIST

Water Lilies	Flowering period	Color	Depth	Spread
Nymphaea 'Ellisiana'	Summer	Red	16 to 24 inches (40 to 60 cm)	2 to 3 feet (60 to 90 cm)
N. 'Froebeli'	Summer	Blood-red	16 to 24 inches (40 to 60 cm)	2 to 3 feet (60 to 90 cm)
N. 'Gonnère'	Summer	White, double	18 to 36 inches (45 to 90 cm)	2 to 3 feet (60 to 90 cm)
N. 'Marliacea Albida'	Summer	White	18 to 36 inches (45 to 90 cm)	2 to 4 feet (60 cm to 1.2 m)
N. 'Marliacea Chromatella'	Summer	Yellow, mottled foliage	18 to 36 inches (45 to 90 cm)	2 to 4 feet (60 cm to 1.2 m)
N. 'Pink Sensation'	Summer	Pink	18 to 36 inches (45 to 90 cm)	2 to 3 feet (60 to 90 cm)
N. 'Rose Arey'	Summer	Pink, fragrant	18 to 30 inches (45 to 75 cm)	2 to 3 feet (60 to 90 cm)

Deep-Water Aquatic	Flowering period	Color	Depth	Spread
Aponogeton distachyos	Summer	White, fragrant	12 to 36 inches (30 to 90 cm)	2 to 3 feet (60 to 90 cm)

Marginal Plants	Flowering period	Color	Depth	Spread
Caltha palustris	Spring	Yellow	12 to 24 inches (30 to 60 cm)	1 to 2 feet (30 to 60 cm)
Iris laevigata	Summer	Blue	24 to 36 inches (60 to 90 cm)	1 to 1½ feet (30 to 45 cm)
Pontederia cordata	Summer	Blue	24 to 36 inches (60 to 90 cm)	1 to 1½ feet (30 to 45 cm)
Schoenoplectus lacustris	Summer	Dark green foliage	24 to 36 inches (60 to 90 cm)	1 to 1½ feet (30 to 45 cm)
Typha minima	Summer	Brown poker	18 inches (45 cm)	1 foot (30 cm)

Submerged Aquatics	Flowering period	Color	Depth	Spread
Elodea canadensis	Semievergreen foliage	Dark green	6 inches to 5 feet (15 cm to 1.5 m)	N/A
Lagarosiphon major	Crispy foliage	Dark green	6 inches to 5 feet (15 cm to 1.5 m)	*(Impossible to give accurate estimates)*
Potamogeton crispus	Crispy translucent foliage	Bronze-green	6 inches to 3⅓ feet (15 cm to 1 m)	

Bog Garden Plants	Flowering period	Color	Depth	Spread
Astilbe 'White Gloria'	Summer	White plumes	24 to 30 inches (60 to 75 cm)	1½ to 2 feet (45 to 60 cm)
Hosta undulata 'Albomarginata'	Summer	Lilac/foliage variegated	24 to 30 inches (60 to 75 cm)	1½ to 2 feet (45 to 60 cm)
Iris ensata	Summer	Deep purple	24 to 30 inches (60 to 75 cm)	1½ to 2 feet (45 to 60 cm)
Primula aurantiaca	Early summer	Orange	24 to 36 inches (60 to 90 cm)	1½ to 2 feet (45 to 60 cm)
Primula pulverulenta	Early summer	Deep red	24 to 36 inches (60 to 90 cm)	1½ to 2 feet (45 to 60 cm)
Rheum palmatum	Summer	Cream/handsome foliage	5 to 6 feet (1.5 to 1.8 m)	3 to 5 feet (1 to 1.5 m)

planting in water features

The planting of aquatic plants takes place during spring and summer. It is important to use a properly prepared aquatic planting compost or a good quality heavy garden soil that has not recently been enriched with organic matter or artificial fertilizer. A slow-release fertilizer in either tablet or sachet form should be pushed into the soil next to each plant. Do not add a general fertilizer to the aquatic compost in the pot—plant nutrients distributed freely throughout the growing medium will leach out into the water and lead to green water problems.

Planting in containers is also wise, especially in formal circumstances where containment of the plant in a given area is desirable not only for practical reasons but also aesthetic ones. Aquatic planting baskets are of latticework construction in order to permit gaseous exchange between pool and plant. Do not grow aquatic plants in solid containers because they will deteriorate rapidly.

It is also possible to grow aquatic plants in hessian rolls filled with compost. Sometimes manufactured rolls of hessian and coir are available. These are excellent for disguising the edge of the pool where it meets the garden. Planted with aquatic plants and laid along the marginal shelf, they provide a wonderfully colorful, sustainable barrier.

Every three to four years, aquatic plants require lifting, dividing, and replanting if they are to retain their vigor. This should ideally be undertaken during the spring or early summer. When replanting, always use the smaller, younger, outside portions of a clump.

PLANTING A WATER LILY

1 *Use a proper latticework planting basket with aquatic planting compost and well-washed pea gravel. The water lily should be strong and healthy with a vigorous rootstock and fresh leaves. Plant in spring.*

2 *Cut away the foliage and fibrous roots. Because the water lily plant has been disturbed, these will die back anyway. The crown will then resprout vigorously when potted.*

3 *Fill the container to within about an inch of the top with aquatic planting compost or good, clean, well-sieved, heavy garden soil.*

4 *Plant the water lily crown in the center of the basket with just the nose and small shoots protruding. Water thoroughly to drive out the air.*

5 *Cover the compost with well-washed pea gravel. This prevents the compost from escaping and polluting the water. It also restricts the activities of fish, which delight in poking around in the container for aquatic insects.*

Above: *Water lilies make a fine show. If planted during spring, they usually produce a good display during their first season.*

6 *Place the water lily in position in the pond. Because there is no foliage on the plant, it can be placed safely at its final depth. Fresh water lily pads will soon be produced.*

57

stocking a pond with fish

Fish are an important component of most ponds. However, the temptation to introduce them immediately after planting should be resisted for at least a month so that the plants can settle down and become established. If fish are introduced too early, they can disrupt the plants and cloud the water with disturbed compost. Even a generous layer of pea shingle over the surface of the pots will not prevent this from happening.

There is no absolute requirement for fish, although their absence will ensure that the pond becomes a nursery for mosquito larvae. Aquatic insect pests are also best controlled by fish, so even when you have no particular interest in keeping them, a few are desirable on purely practical grounds.

There are no hard and fast rules as to how many fish a pond can accommodate. It has much more to do with the total length of the fish population with respect to the amount of open surface area. The stocking rate that best allows for growth and development is 2 inches (5 cm) of fish to every 1 square foot (0.095 m²). This does not refer to the total surface area of the pond but to open water uncluttered by marginal plants.

Most hardy ornamental fish live happily together. Goldfish in their various varieties are particularly pleasing, especially the brightly colored shubunkins. Comet-tailed varieties are very hardy, but the fantail and veiltail forms must have water at least 2 feet (60 cm) deep at one point in the pond in order to overwinter satisfactorily in those parts of the world where winter temperatures may drop down to 14° to 5°F (10° to 15°C below zero).

Golden orfe are an attractive proposition, especially where there is moving water, because they love to sport in the spray. There is also a silver variety, and together with golden rudd they make a trio of the finest alternatives to goldfish.

In a well-balanced pond, there is no need to feed fish, but many formal ponds are not well balanced, and feeding is beneficial. Feeding is also attractive for the gardener, because then the fish become tame and come to the surface when food is offered. Feed at the same point in the pool to encourage their prompt appearance, and give no more food than they can clear up in 20 minutes. Any food left uneaten should be netted out, because decomposition of this residue will lead to the buildup of ammonia in the pond.

INTRODUCING ORNAMENTAL FISH

1 *When purchased, fish are usually in a bag containing a small amount of water and blown up with air. Float the bag on the surface of the water for 20 minutes to allow the water temperatures to equalize.*

2 *The fish can then be gently coaxed out of the plastic bag into the pool. Do not worry if they are not seen for a day or two. Once settled in, they will reappear again.*

FISH TREATMENTS

1 *Add a protective disinfectant such as methylene blue to a bowl of water to create a bath.*

2 *Swim new fish in the bath for a minute as a precaution before introducing them to the pool.*

3 *There are various pond treatments that can improve water conditions and help to prevent disease outbreaks.*

4 *Mix in a bucket according to instructions; pour from the bucket into the pool and distribute freely in the water.*

Below: *The constant monitoring of fish health is vital when there is a large population. With Koi carp and other specialist fish, medication may be administered through the pump and filter.*

coping with physical problems

A number of practical tasks are necessary to ensure the smooth running of the formal pond, especially so when moving water is part of the feature. Although modern submersible pumps are fine examples of modern engineering, they do require regular maintenance. They should be removed periodically—at least monthly—to check the input. This has a simple filter with a removable cover, which makes for easy washing out.

As the winter approaches, remove the pump from the pond and replace it with a pond heater. This ensures a small ice-free area, which permits the escape of accumulated gases caused by the decomposition of plant material and leaves and prevents asphyxiation of the fish. When the pump has been removed, separate it into its component parts and wash it thoroughly. It should be stored in a dry place for the winter.

It is useful to clean the filter at least annually, depending on the type used. Although a biological filter will digest much of the waste organic materials that pass through it naturally, its efficiency is often impaired by accumulated debris. A biological filter is generally better cleaned just before the spring season so that the desirable bacteria can reestablish quickly, whereas a mechanical filter should be washed out regularly during the summer months and then again just before winter.

Occasionally a pond springs a leak. For lined ponds, there are special repair kits available to ensure a well-patched repair, but for polyethylene liners or plastic preformed pools, repair is more difficult. Fiberglass pools can easily be repaired with a motor repair kit, and concrete fractures with a quick-setting cement mixed with a waterproofer, after the flaw has been chiseled around.

CLEANING THE PUMP

Make sure that the fountain control assembly is clear of algae and other debris.

1 *The pump is likely to be coated in algae and various sorts of organic debris if it has been in the pool for some time. Remove any clinging weed by hand and place the pump in a bowl of clean water.*

2 *Pull the pump apart. The filter section is usually easily detached from the pump motor, and it will contain a sponge with collected debris. Wash this out thoroughly, and replace the filter.*

3 *The pump should be thoroughly scrubbed and dried. Modern submersible pumps rarely require any technical maintenance. If something does go wrong, it is usually quicker and easier simply to replace the unit.*

REPAIRING A LINER

1 *Scrub the liner clean in the area around the tear to ensure that the patch will stick to the liner properly.*

2 *Cut a piece of special repair tape to length, making sure that there is sufficient overlap to guarantee a strong bond.*

3 *Firmly apply the patch, ensuring that the adhesive makes firm contact. Let it dry for at least a day before reintroducing water.*

Right: *To keep a water garden looking good year-round, it is important to follow a regular maintenance regimen.*

maintaining the ecobalance

It is important that the ecosystem of a pond is in balance. Ideally this should be achieved by the correct ratio of plants to fish, although in a formal pool where the reflective quality of the water is of major importance, ideals have to be sacrificed and artificial methods used to ensure that the water chemistry and clarity are satisfactory.

A natural balance is achieved when there are sufficient submerged plants established in the pond to mop up excessive nutrients in the water. This makes life difficult for single-celled, water-discoloring algae, which can turn the pond to a consistency of pea soup. Generally the more submerged aquatic plants there are, the better, but a minimum stocking rate is ten bunches for each square meter of open surface area.

Algae also prosper when the water surface is open to the sun. In many formal ponds, this openness is desirable—a glassy, unpunctuated stillness being precisely what is required. If surface cover by water lily pads or floating plants is not desired, then chemicals have to be added to control the algae. Where plants are desired, then one-third of the surface area of the pond should be covered by foliage in order to reduce the amount of sunlight falling beneath the water.

Barley straw is a valuable long-term solution to algal problems, provided that it is replaced three or four times in the growing season. The slowly decomposing straw mops up the nutrients that the green algae would otherwise use. It is important to replace the barley straw before it starts to decompose or else

Above: *A well-balanced pool where the ecosystem is working well. The key to success is to have a sufficient complement of plants and a small population of fish.*

the nutrients are returned to the water. Special barley straw bags for suspending in the water can be purchased from most garden centers, although it is quite simple to make them from barley straw and garden netting.

Marginal plants make no major contribution to the balance of the pond, but they are vital for creating the right aesthetic effect. With a formal pond, reeds, rushes, and sedges play an important visual role.

Apart from the use of algaecides, netting filamentous algae or twirling it around a stick and pulling it out of the pond is the only realistic control. When large quantities of blanket-weed are killed with an algaecide, it is still important to remove it before decomposition sets in and the water becomes polluted.

COPING WITH ALGAE

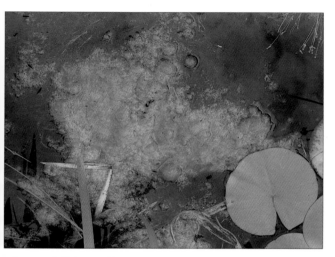

Above: Of all the troublesome algae, it is the filamentous kinds like blanket- and flannelweed that cause the greatest distress. Even when nutrients are at their minimum, these advanced forms can survive.

1 *Barley straw provides a solution to many algal problems by mopping up excess nutrients, which algae feed on, during decomposition. Barley straw decomposes very slowly.*

2 *Take some lengths of barley straw and bend and twist them into a ball. It is also possible to use other cereal straws, as well as lavender trimmings, to similar effect.*

3 *Take a small square of garden netting and tie the straw into a ball. The useful life of a barley straw ball is about four months during the summer.*

4 *Place the barley straw ball toward the edge of the pool and hide it discreetly. Attach a string to it so that once it starts to decompose it can be easily retrieved and removed from the pool.*

index

Photo Credits

Eric Crichton: 9 bottom, 17 bottom (design: Yves St Laurent, RHS Chelsea 1997), 20 left (design: Arabella Lennox-Boyd, Evening Standard, RHS Chelsea 1998), 21 (design: Arabella Lennox-Boyd, RHS Chelsea 1995), 35 (Wyevale Garden Centres, RHS Chelsea 2001), 37 (RHS Chelsea 1993), 39 (Mrs. Daphne Foulsham), 41 (*Country Living* Garden, RHS Chelsea 1993), 48 (Mitsubishi, RHS Hampton Court 2001), 49 (RHS Chelsea 1994), 57, 62 (design: Paul Dyer, The Very Interested Landscape Company, RHS Chelsea 2000). **John Glover:** 8, 9 top, 11 (design: Susy Smith), 13 (design: Susy Smith), 15 (design: Hiroshi Nanamori), 17 top (design: Michael Miller, RHS Chelsea 2001), 18 (design: Andy Sturgeon, RHS Chelsea 2001), 27 left (design: Fiona Lawrenson, RHS Chelsea 1998), 27 right (design: Clare Whitehouse, RHS Hampton Court 1995), 29, 40, 47 (design: Mark Walker, RHS Chelsea 1995), 61 (RHS Chelsea 1992). **S. and O. Mathews:** 1, 19 right, 23, 26, 51, 59. **Clive Nichols Garden Pictures:** 3 (Stourton House, Wiltshire), 4 (design: Carole Vincent, Blue Circle, RHS Chelsea 2001), 6 (design: Andy Sturgeon, Circ Garden, RHS Chelsea 2001), 7 (design: Mark Walker, RHS Chelsea 2000), 10 (design: James van Sweden), 10–11 (design: Claus Scheinert), 12 (design: Christian Wright), 14 (Spidergarden.com, RHS Chelsea 2000), 16–17 (design: Chris Gregory, RHS Chelsea 1999), 19 left (design: Michael Balston, RHS Chelsea 1999), 22 (design: Deborah Lewis), 24 (design: Shelia Stedman), 24–25 (Tintinhull Gardens, Somerset), 33 (Wollerton Old Hall, Shropshire), 43 (Gordon White, Texas). **Neil Sutherland:** 5, 20 right, 44, 53.